45TH PARALLEL PRESS

Published in the United States of America by Cherry Lake Publishing Group
Ann Arbor, Michigan
www.cherrylakepublishing.com

Reading Adviser: Beth Walker Gambro, MS, Ed., Reading Consultant, Yorkville, IL
Content Adviser: Mark Richards, Ph.D., Professor, Dept. of Political Science, Grand Valley State University, Allendale, MI
Book Designer: Frame25 Productions

Photo Credits: © AP Photo/Stephan Savoia, File, cover, title page; © LightField Studios/Shutterstock, 5; © Orlowski Designs LLC/Shutterstock, 7; James Peale, CC0, via Wikimedia Commons, 9; Official White House photographer, Public domain, via Wikimedia Commons, 13; Bill Hrybyk for NASA, Public domain, via Wikimedia Commons, 17; Governo do Estado de São Paulo, CC BY 2.0, via Wikimedia Commons, 19; © Tinseltown/Shutterstock, 21; U.S. Air Force photo/Staff Sgt. Michael R. Holzworth, Public domain, via Wikimedia Commons, 25; Harris & Ewing, Library of Congress, Prints and Photographs Division, 29; © Rosamar/Shutterstock, 31

Copyright © 2025 by Cherry Lake Publishing Group

All rights reserved. No part of this book may be reproduced or utilized in any form or by any means without written permission from the publisher.

45th Parallel Press is an imprint of Cherry Lake Publishing Group.

Library of Congress Cataloging-in-Publication Data has been filed and is available at catalog.loc.gov

Cherry Lake Publishing Group would like to acknowledge the work of the Partnership for 21st Century Learning, a Network of Battelle for Kids. Please visit Battelle for Kids online for more information.

Note from publisher: Websites change regularly, and their future contents are outside of our control. Supervise children when conducting any recommended online searches for extended learning opportunities.

Printed in the United States of America

ABOUT THE AUTHOR

Dr. Virginia Loh-Hagan is an author and educator. She is currently the Director of the Asian Pacific Islander Desi American (APIDA) Center at San Diego State University and the Co-Executive Director of The Asian American Education Project. She lives in San Diego with her very tall husband and very naughty dogs.

CONTENTS

Introduction 4

Chapter 1: **George Washington (1732–1799)** 8

Chapter 2: **P. T. Barnum (1810–1891)** 10

Chapter 3: **Ronald Reagan (1911–2004)** 12

Chapter 4: **Shirley Temple (1928–2014)** 14

Chapter 5: **George Takei (born 1937)** 16

Chapter 6: **Arnold Schwarzenegger (born 1947)** 18

Chapter 7: **Caitlyn Jenner (born 1949)** 20

Chapter 8: **Jesse Ventura (born 1951)** 22

Chapter 9: **Kid Rock (born 1971)** 24

Chapter 10: **Ben Savage (born 1980)** 26

Do Your Part! 28

Glossary, Learn More, Index 32

INTRODUCTION

The United States is a top world power. It's not ruled by kings or queens. It's a **democracy**. A democracy is a system of government. It means "rule by the people." People **elect** their leaders. They choose leaders by voting.

Leaders **represent** the people who voted for them. They speak for them. They make decisions for them. That's why voting is so important. By voting, we choose our leaders.

Candidates run for **public office**. Public office is a government position. Candidates are people who want to be elected to certain positions. They run **campaigns**. They do this before an election. Campaigns are planned activities. Some campaigns are easy. Some are hard. And some are full of drama.

Many public office positions have terms. Terms are periods of time. This means there are many elections.

Every U.S. citizen has the right to be elected. There are many public offices. Each office has different requirements. Age is one requirement. Most candidates must be at least 18 years old. Another requirement is **residency**. Residency is where one lives. Most candidates must live in the area they serve.

Running for U.S. president has several specific rules. One rule is that candidates must be U.S. citizens. Another is that they must be at least 35 years old. They must have lived in the U.S. for 14 years.

Some candidates are young. Some are old. Some are unknown. Some are **celebrities**. Celebrities are famous people. They are well-known. There have been many candidates in U.S. history. This book features the celebrity candidates!

Each state has its own election laws. Each city has its own election laws.

CHAPTER ONE
GEORGE WASHINGTON
(1732–1799)

George Washington was the first U.S. president. He got 100 percent of the votes. He's the only president to do that. He's known as the "Father of the Nation." He's also called "America's First Celebrity."

Before taking office, he was a war hero. He fought in the Revolutionary War (1775–1783). He led the army to victory. Poets wrote about him. They said he was a Greek god. Artists painted him like a Roman hero. Washington got tired of sitting for paintings. He said, "I am so heartily tired of…these kinds of people…" These artists were like today's **paparazzi**. Paparazzi are photographers. They snap photos of famous people.

George Washington was tall. He was good at sports. He camped. He hunted. He was a good dancer. He was popular. He was well-liked.

CHAPTER TWO
P. T. BARNUM
(1810–1891)

P. T. Barnum was famous for his circus. He said, "I am a showman by profession." He built theaters. He built museums. He made the prices low. He wanted working people to enjoy things. He knew how to entertain people. This helped him in politics.

In 1865, Barnum was elected to the Connecticut General Assembly. He served several terms. In 1867, he ran for Congress. He lost to his 3rd cousin. In 1875, he served as mayor of Bridgeport, Connecticut. He improved the water supply. He brought gas lighting to streets. He helped build a hospital.

Barnum said nothing "ever kept me from the **polls**." Polls means voting.

WORLD AFFAIRS

All countries have leaders. We should know who world leaders are. We're connected to what happens around the world. Other countries also have celebrity candidates. Manny Pacquiao (born 1978) is from the Philippines. The Philippines is a country in the Pacific Ocean. It is in Southeast Asia. Pacquiao is a professional boxer. He's won world championships. He did this in 8 different weight classes. He's the only boxer to have done so. He entered politics in 2007. He ran for election to the House of Representatives of the Philippines. He lost his first race. He ran again in 2010. He won. In 2016, he was elected as a senator. In 2021, he retired from boxing. He wanted to focus on politics. In 2022, he ran for president of the Philippines. Ten other people ran. Pacquiao was the youngest candidate. He lost. He was in 3rd place. He said, "I am a fighter. And I will always be a fighter inside and outside the ring."

CHAPTER THREE
RONALD REAGAN
(1911–2004)

Ronald Reagan was the 40th U.S. president. He was also governor of California. Before that, he was an actor. He acted in more than 50 movies. He's known for his **western** movies. Westerns are cowboy movies.

His first big role was playing George Gipp (1895–1920). Gipp was a college football player. In the movie, Reagan said, "Win one for the Gipper." After that, he became known as "The Gipper."

Reagan also hosted *General Electric Theater*. This show aired every Sunday night. It featured various stories. Reagan introduced each story. He also acted in the show. The show made Reagan more appealing. People liked him. This probably helped him get elected.

Nancy Reagan was married to Ronald Reagan.
She was the first lady. She was also an actor.

CHAPTER FOUR

SHIRLEY TEMPLE
(1928–2014)

Shirley Temple was a child actress. She sang. She danced. She was a big star. She started in movies at age 3. She acted in more than 40 movies. She was known for her curly hair. She was known for her dimples.

Temple ran for office. She did this in 1967. She ran for Congress. She wanted to be the first woman to represent California. She said, "I think men are fine and here to stay. But I have a hunch that it wouldn't hurt to have a woman's viewpoint expressed…"

She didn't win. But she became active in politics. She served as a U.S. **ambassador**. Ambassadors represent the United States in foreign countries.

THE IDEAL CANDIDATE

Ideal candidates are role models. Clint Eastwood (born 1930) is a famous actor. He often plays tough guys. He lived in Carmel-by-the-Sea. This town is in northern California. Eastwood wanted to build office spaces. The city council denied his request. Eastwood fought back. He decided to make changes. He ran for mayor in 1986. He won. He got more than 70 percent of the vote. He earned $200 per month as mayor. He donated that money to the local youth center. Carmel-by-the-Sea had unusual laws. It banned eating ice cream on the streets. It banned individual mailboxes. It banned street signs. Eastwood thought this was silly. He thought the city was stuck in the past. He changed the laws. Now people can eat ice cream in peace. Eastwood did more. He added public bathrooms at the beach. He created beach walkways. He added more tourist parking spots. He expanded the library. He wrote a weekly newspaper column. He took his role seriously.

CHAPTER FIVE
GEORGE TAKEI
(BORN 1937)

George Takei is an actor. He's most famous for the TV show *Star Trek*. He played Hikaru Sulu. He's known for his deep voice.

In 1973, he ran for office. He wanted a seat on the Los Angeles City Council. Five people ran. Takei lost. He came in second. But the mayor appointed him to positions. Takei helped plan the L.A. subway system. He even left a movie set to vote.

Other candidates thought Takei had an unfair advantage. He was on TV a lot. A local TV station had to stop showing *Star Trek*.

In 2017, Takei said he was running for Congress. A few hours later, he said it was an April Fools' joke.

George Takei is also an author and activist. He fights for Asian American rights. He fights for gay rights.

CHAPTER SIX

ARNOLD SCHWARZENEGGER
(BORN 1947)

Arnold Schwarzenegger was a professional **bodybuilder**. Bodybuilders exercise a lot. They make their muscles bigger. Professionals compete in contests. Schwarzenegger won the Mr. Universe title. He won other awards.

He's famous for other things. He's an actor. He's known for his action movies. He was in the *Terminator* movies. He was also governor of California. He became known as "The Governator."

Some voters want him to run for U.S. president. But he can't. He was born in Austria. Austria is in Europe. Schwarzenegger became a U.S. citizen in 1983. He said, "I owe everything to America."

Arnold Schwarzenegger said he still works out every day.

CHAPTER SEVEN

CAITLYN JENNER
(BORN 1949)

Caitlyn Jenner was born William Bruce Jenner. Jenner was in the Olympics. She won a gold medal. She's also a TV personality. She's in reality shows. Reality shows usually film ordinary people.

In 2015, she came out as a **transgender woman**. Transgender women are assigned male at birth. They have a female gender identity.

In 2021, Jenner ran for governor of California. She tweeted, "I'm in." She called herself an "outsider." During the campaign, she left the United States. She went to Australia. She was in a TV show.

Jenner came in 13th place. She got 1 percent of the vote.

Caitlyn Jenner married into the famous Kardashian family.

CHAPTER EIGHT
JESSE VENTURA
(BORN 1951)

Jesse "The Body" Ventura is from Minnesota. His real name is James George Janos. Ventura was a professional wrestler. He played a tough guy. He played a beach bodybuilder. He starred in movies. He starred in TV shows. He had a radio show. He wrote books.

Ventura used his fame to get votes. He was elected mayor of Brooklyn Park, Minnesota. He was also elected governor of Minnesota. His voters would say, "My governor can beat up your governor."

He thought about running for U.S. president in 2020. But he decided against it.

HOT-BUTTON ISSUE

Hot-button issues refer to tough topics. People have strong emotions. They take sides. Not everyone thinks celebrities should run for office. Celebrities use their fame to win. Voters recognize their names. They think they know them because of their fame. Celebrities live different lives. Some people think they're out of touch with real issues. They don't trust them to make laws for them. They don't trust them to know about politics.

Celebrities can play an important role. They can support candidates. They can spread awareness. Tom Hanks is a famous actor. He's known for playing good guys. People have asked him to run for U.S. president. He said, "Just because I'm an actor, I can give a good speech…But the concept of actually voting for someone just because they can do that? Then Monty Hall could have been president…" Monty Hall (1921–2017) was a famous game show host. Hanks thinks candidates should be more than just famous.

CHAPTER NINE
KID ROCK
(BORN 1971)

Kid Rock is a rock star. He was born Robert James Ritchie. He taught himself music. He got into the hip-hop scene. He performs rap. He performs country rock. He is also a **deejay**. Deejays play songs. They mix sounds.

Kid Rock likes politics. He has supported candidates. He has spoken out on issues. In 2017, he shared a photo. The photo was of a yard sign. The yard sign read, "Kid Rock for U.S. Senate." Kid Rock made a website. He sold shirts. He sold other things. Everyone thought he was running to represent Michigan. Later, he said he wasn't running. He said it was a joke.

Kid Rock has toured with the United Service Organizations (USO). He played music for members of the U.S. Armed Forces.

CHAPTER TEN
BEN SAVAGE
(BORN 1980)

Ben Savage is a child actor. He starred in *Boy Meets World*. This show ran for 7 years. He stopped acting. He went to Stanford University. He got a degree in political science. He worked for a U.S. senator.

In 2022, Savage ran for a seat on the West Hollywood City Council. He lost. In 2023, he announced a run for Congress. He wants to expand union rights. He wants to build cheaper housing. He wants to end gun violence. He said, "It's time for new and passionate leaders who can help move our country forward."

FACT-CHECK

It's important to check facts. Facts must be correct. Here are some fun facts about celebrity candidates:

- Volodymyr Zelensky (born 1978) is Ukrainian. Ukraine is in eastern Europe. It borders Russia. Zelensky is its 6th president. Before, he was an actor. He was a comedian. He had played the president on TV. Then he became president in real life.

- Celebrity candidates can use their fame. They're well-known. They have media attention. But they often lose in elections. They tend not to have support from a major political party. They tend to raise less money than other candidates. They tend to lack experience in politics.

- Short ballots have a few candidates. Long ballots have a lot of candidates. Celebrities win on long ballots. They lose on short ballots.

- Celebrities endorse candidates. They help candidates win. They get people to vote. Warren Harding (1865–1923) was the 29th U.S. president. He was one of the first to have celebrity endorsers.

DO YOUR PART!

U.S. citizens have 2 special rights. Only U.S. citizens can vote in federal elections. Only U.S. citizens can run for **federal office**. Federal office means a national office. It's different from state and local offices.

U.S. citizens have many other rights. But they also have duties. The most powerful is the duty to vote. Voting is how people choose leaders. It's how people make changes. It's how people promote their ideas. Those elected make the laws. They make policies. They make the rules. They work for voters.

U.S. citizens can vote at age 18. But people are never too young to get involved in democracy.

Many groups of people have fought for the right to vote. Women in the U.S. won the right to vote in 1920. Then, the Voting Rights Act of 1965 guaranteed the right to vote regardless of race.

Citizens vote for candidates. They get a **ballot**. The ballot has a list of candidates. Voters must choose the best person for the job. Here are some ideas to learn more about candidates:

★ Look beyond the fame. Think about what they stand for. Think about what issues they'll fight for.

★ Learn everything about the candidate. Do an online search. Listen to their speeches. Read everything you can.

★ Volunteer to work in election campaigns. Learn how the candidates work. Learn how they treat people.

Everyone can do their part. Being a good citizen is hard work. But the work is worth it. Your vote is your voice.

Most elections will send a voter's guide.
This guide has information about each candidate.

GLOSSARY

ambassador (am-BA-suh-dur) a person appointed to represent their country's government in another country

ballot (BA-luht) a piece of paper or electronic device on which voters enter their choices

bodybuilder (BAH-dee-bil-dur) a person who strengthens and enlarges their muscles through exercise

campaigns (kam-PAYNZ) organized courses of action to achieve a goal such as winning an election

candidates (KAN-duh-dayts) people who want to be elected to certain positions

celebrities (suh-LEH-bruh-teez) famous people, especially in the entertainment business

deejay (DEE-jay) a person who plays music on the radio or at a party or club

democracy (dih-MAH-kruh-see) a system of government led by voters, often through elected representatives

elect (ih-LEKT) to choose someone to hold public office by voting

federal office (FEH-druhl AW-fuhs) an elected position in the national government

paparazzi (pah-puh-RAHT-see) photographers who try to get photos of celebrities

polls (POHLZ) places where people go to vote

public office (PUH-blik AW-fuhs) government position established by law

represent (reh-prih-ZENT) to speak or act for another person or group

residency (REH-zuh-duhn-see) an official place where a person lives

transgender woman (trans-JEN-duhr WUH-muhn) woman who was assigned male at birth but who has a female gender identity

western (WEH-sturn) a film or TV show about cowboys in western North America in the late 19th and early 20th centuries

LEARN MORE

Burns, Ken. *Grover Cleveland, Again!: A Treasury of American Presidents.* New York: Knopf Books for Young Readers, 2016.

Leslie, Jay. *Who Did It First? 50 Politicians, Activists, and Entrepreneurs Who Revolutionized the World.* New York: Henry Holt and Company, 2020.

Yacka, Douglas. *What Is a Presidential Election?* New York: Penguin Workshop, 2020.

INDEX

actors, 12–13, 14, 15, 16–17, 18–19, 22, 23, 26, 27
ambassadors, 14
athletes, 11, 18, 20, 22

Barnum, P.T., 10
businesspeople, 10

candidates
    qualifications, 6, 8, 18, 23, 27, 30–31
    voter decisions, 4, 23, 27, 30–31
citizens' rights, 4, 6, 28–30
congressional campaigns, 10, 11, 14, 26

Eastwood, Clint, 15
election laws, 6, 7, 28–29
endorsements, 27

fame, 6, 23, 27, 30
gubernatorial elections

losing candidates, 20–21
winning candidates, 12, 18, 22

Hanks, Tom, 23
Harding, Warren, 27

images, of candidates, 8–9

Jenner, Caitlyn, 20–21
joke campaigns, 16, 24

Kid Rock, 24–25

local leaders, 10, 15, 16, 22

mayors, 10, 15, 22
military leaders, 8–9
musicians, 24–25

Pacquiao, Manny, 11
Philippines, 11

presidential campaigns
    losing candidates, 11
    rules, 6, 18
    winning candidates, 8–9, 12, 27

Reagan, Nancy, 13
Reagan, Ronald, 12, 13

Savage, Ben, 26

Takei, George, 16–17
Temple, Shirley, 14

Ventura, Jesse, 22
voting and voting rights, 4, 5, 7, 28–31

Washington, George, 8–9

Zelensky, Volodymyr, 27